TULSA CITY-COUNTY LIBRARY

D0857562

CEYA

20 GREAT
CAREER-BUILDING
ACTIVITIES USING
TUMBLR®

SUSAN HENNEBERG

ROSEN
PUBLISHING®

New York

Published in 2017 by The Rosen Publishing Group, Inc.
29 East 21st Street, New York, NY 10010

Copyright © 2017 by The Rosen Publishing Group, Inc.

First Edition

All rights reserved. No part of this book may be reproduced in any form without permission in writing from the publisher, except by a reviewer.

Library of Congress Cataloging-in-Publication Data

Names: Henneberg, Susan, author.
Title: 20 great career-building activities using Tumblr / Susan Henneberg.
Other titles: Twenty great career-building activities using Tumblr
Description: First edition. | New York : Rosen Publishing, 2017. | Series: Social media career building | Includes bibliographical references and index.
Identifiers: LCCN 2016018201 | ISBN 9781508172666 (library bound)
Subjects: LCSH: Blogs—Vocational guidance—Juvenile literature. | Tumblr (Electronic resource)—Juvenile literature.
Classification: LCC TK5105.8884 .H46 2017 | DDC 650.10285/6752—dc23
LC record available at https://lccn.loc.gov/2016018201

Manufactured in China

Reference to and use of Tumblr docs not imply endorsement or sponsorship, and our publication is for informational purposes only relative to possible uses of the Tumblr site.

CONTENTS

who are you really?

So begins a poem written by college student Madisen Kuhn, one of more than two hundred poems posted on her blog on Tumblr. The blogger Ava Willford is one of the sixty-five thousand followers who got to know who Kuhn was through her poetry, journals, YouTube videos, and photography. Kuhn, known as m.k., poured out her insecurities, flashed her quirky humor, and shared her deep religious beliefs. She showed off new hairstyles and colors, reflected on her growth and evolution, and shared her anxieties about starting college. As her popularity grew, m.k. became a presence on other social media sites such as Instagram and Twitter. Then she published her first book of poetry, *Eighteen*.

Madisen Kuhn is not the first published author who began a road to success on Tumblr. In 2010 photographer Brandon Stanton began a project on Tumblr to create a photographic blog of New York City. Each day, he posted a photo of someone he came across on the streets of New York. He acquired hundreds, then thousands, and now millions of followers. He also attracted

Tumblr blogger Brandon Stanton has posted thousands of photographs of ordinary New York residents for his *Humans of New York* project.

the attention of an editor at St. Martin's Press. His first book, *Humans of New York*, was published in 2013. It quickly became a best seller, and Brandon Stanton was recognized as one of *Time* magazine's "30 People Under 30 Changing the World."

These aren't the only bloggers who became published authors. Tumblr blogger Emily Trunko also earned book deals with her projects *Dear My Blank* and *The Last Message Received*. She receives up to one hundred letters a day from people wanting to share letters never sent or stories of friends never seen again. Another blogger, Christopher Weingarten, capitalized on his popular site to publish *Hipster Puppies* in 2010.

While none of these writers and photographers began their blogs with the intention of publishing a book, their original ideas, thoughtful posts, commitment to maintaining their presence, and connection to other bloggers brought them recognition and success. Talented teens and young adults are using social media to help themselves move toward their goals, whether in higher education, as part of a professional life, or for a personal cause. Tumblr creates the perfect platform to begin this process.

What appeal does Tumblr possess to attract over two hundred million bloggers publishing eighty million posts per day? Users say that it is easy, with only a few fields to fill out to register. It is quick to use, too. As a microblogging site, most posts are just a photo, a paragraph or two, a scanned image, or a link to a short audio clip. At a 2013 advertisers' conference, Tumblr founder and CEO David Karp said that Tumblr users spent longer per visit than any other social media site.

Colleges have found Tumblr, as have businesses and nonprofits. It has become the "cool" place to host creative portfolios. It is the place where publishers find their next best-selling author, design and animation studios discover new talent, comic artists amass huge, appreciative audiences, and socially minded activists direct attention to important movements.

Like Madisen Kuhn, thousands of teens and young adults have discovered themselves through the power of regularly posting one's hopes, dreams, and best work. On Tumblr, bloggers put themselves and their projects in front of their peers, college admissions officers, potential employers, clients and customers, and the world. They become inspired and encouraged by their fellow bloggers. Tumblr has enormous potential for those who are willing to take the time to learn how to use it in the most productive ways.

CHAPTER ONE

Changing the Way We Blog

L ike so many popular internet applications, Tumblr was created by a self-taught, college-age computer programmer who couldn't find the right program to fit his needs. In 2007, David Karp was looking for a website on which to write short blog entries. He discovered a type of micro-blogging platform known as "tumblelogs." He couldn't find a site that just specialized in these short form blogs, where users could share posts of just a few sentences easily. Seeing an opportunity, David and his partner Marco Arment created a tumblelog website and called it Tumblr.

David Karp grew up fascinated by technology and the internet. He taught himself how to use hypertext markup language (HTML) when he was eleven years old. He was soon creating his own websites. At age fourteen, he landed an internship at Federator Studios, which specialized in animation. By age seventeen David was working his first real job, creating an internet forum for a website where parents could discuss topics relating to children. When the website was sold, David decided to strike out on his own. He wanted to be an entrepreneur, so he started his own internet consulting company. He called it Davidville.

David and his company began earning money right away. He was so busy that he dropped out of high school and decided he didn't need to go to college. He and Marco launched Tumblr 3.0 in November 2007, after working out the bugs of previous versions. It was an immediate success. Within the first two weeks, over seventy-five thousand new users had registered for the site.

David Karp created the first version of Tumblr while still in his teens. He sold the site to Yahoo for $1 billion in 2013.

Tumblr grew fast. Users loved the site because it was easy, creative, and free. However, David and Marco needed more resources to keep the platform growing and innovating. They needed more employees and more technology. They did not want to make users pay for the site, nor did they want to crowd the site with advertising. In 2013 they made the decision to sell Tumblr to the giant internet company Yahoo! with the condition that David stay on as chief executive officer (CEO).

Today Tumblr is one of the top ten social networking sites in the world and one of the fastest growing. In March 2016, Tumblr reported that it had over 280 million users and was hosting over 130 billion blog posts. Although the United States has the highest user count, Tumblr is popular in the United Kingdom, Canada, Brazil, and Russia. Users visit the site an average of six times each day. It is most popular with high school and young adult populations. Over half of Tumblr account holders have college degrees. Most of the activity on Tumblr happens in the evening hours.

Bloggers choose Tumblr because it is so versatile. It is known for a variety of types of multimedia posts. Users can feature text, photos, links, audio files, or video. For longer posts, bloggers can show the first section and hide the rest for viewers to read if they want. Tumblr allows users to customize their site with themes, sidebars, and social buttons. Users can be public, or private and anonymous.

Because of all its features, Tumblr has played an important role in creating success for its users. Bloggers have used Tumblr as part of their college

THE IMPACT OF BLOGGING

The word "blog" is a mash-up of the words "web" and "log." People use blogs for many different reasons. Some treat their blogs like a diary, documenting the events of their lives for others to see. There are travel, hobby, wedding, first job, and parenting blogs. Some use blogs to promote their work, hoping to generate interest in their product. Blogging has become an important news source for activists all over the world who need to share information about events in their countries. Some people credit blogs for sparking popular uprisings and revolutions in such countries as Tunisia, Egypt, and Libya.

Egyptian activists organized their protests against their government using social media sites such as Tumblr.

applications. They add their Tumblr addresses to their résumés. They promote their talents, skills, and achievements, as well as their entrepreneurial activities. They express their passions and creativity in a fun, original way for others to find. They learn new skills, make new friends, and open new doors to opportunity.

People who choose microblogging have some of the same goals as bloggers. They want, however, a shorter, faster medium in which to express their ideas and share their passions. Tumblr is just one of many microblogging sites available for free to bloggers over the age of thirteen. Posting on one of these platforms takes less time than a blogging site and can be done on a mobile device. This allows users to post more frequently, which helps build followers. The posts take less time to view and are usually more interactive. Users can comment on, re-blog, and like posts on the fly.

CHAPTER TWO

Creating a Killer Site

Most Tumblr users want to attract, keep, and grow an audience. Successful bloggers advise new users to find a niche, a narrow interest area that will draw specific communities of followers. The niche a new blogger will choose depends on the user's goals. Once a goal is identified, users can exploit all of Tumblr's tools to create a killer site. Users who already have a Tumblr site that they use for fun are better off creating a fresh, new site if they want to use Tumblr to promote their academic, business, or creative projects.

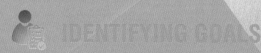

IDENTIFYING GOALS

Most successful bloggers on Tumblr have a narrow focus that aligns with their goals for the site. Photographers want paying assignments, fashion stylists want attention from designers and major brands, and musicians want audiences, gigs, and contracts from major labels. They are promoting themselves to the social media universe.

Bloggers also search for opportunities to grow and improve by learning from other bloggers. Tumblr is a place of give and take. The most resourceful Tumblr users thoughtfully create and choose content for their sites that will help them achieve these objectives.

If your goal is to get into a good college, you might load your site with items that show your interest in a possible major. If you are exploring a medical career, you might search for and re-blog cutting-edge developments or new technologies that get you—and your followers—excited. Budding animators might want to find mentors to help them get to the next level. Time spent reflecting on your goals will pay off in a site that brings you closer to your dreams.

 ## EXPLORE THE SITE

Taking the time to explore Tumblr will provide many benefits. With over fifty million new posts each day, users should be able to find something worthwhile to spend their time on. On your dashboard, known by users as the "dash," is a compass icon that provides several options for exploring the site. You may want to critically examine the sites that attract your attention to figure out how the users put them together. There are many options in terms of designing your site, so poking around will help you determine what is effective.

Like Google, Netflix, and Facebook, Tumblr uses algorithms to recommend content that users might like. These complex mathematical formulas collect information about where users have visited and use this

Tumblr has a variety of resources for students to use for writing classes, research projects, and college searches.

data to suggest new posts. Click on the Recommended icon to see what the Tumblr programmers have chosen for you.

Tumblr engineers also keep an eye on emerging trends. Click on the Trending icon to see a wide-ranging mix of emerging memes and current media obsessions. A meme is an idea that is quickly spread through the

NOT SAFE FOR WORK

Anyone new to Tumblr quickly realizes that there is adult-oriented content. Tumblr has a relaxed policy regarding what it calls not safe for work (NSFW) posts. Many teens have a lot of curiosity about sexually themed content. However, this material has no place on a site you are using to promote yourself. It is easy to block. The first time you enter a term in to the Search window, scroll down to the padlock icon and make sure it is locked. This procedure ensures that posts labeled NSFW will be filtered from dash.

What happens if an adult-themed post turns up in a search? The Tumblr team asks that you flag it by clicking on the three-dot menu at the bottom of the post and let the team know it should be filtered.

internet and social media. Staff Picks allow Tumblr team members to spotlight posts that they thought were particularly interesting, beautiful, clever, or funny. Here you will find posts that you might not come across in your normal browsing, but will make you think in new ways.

Tumblr is most fun and beneficial when users become interactive. Take the time to like posts by clicking on the heart icon. Click the Follow icon to subscribe to the blogger. You can also reblog the post on your own site, or send the blogger a message. The more you interact with fellow bloggers, the more they will interact with you.

CREATE A GREAT SITE

Creating an account on Tumblr is fast and easy. Creating an amazing site will take some time, effort, and a lot of creativity. To sign up, you need to give your email address. Make sure to use an original, hack-proof password so that your account stays safe. While you might be tempted to create a fun, trendy username, this will not help you become professional. Use your real name, with numbers after it if your name is taken. For instance, Aurelia Lucy Marin could choose ALMarin, AureliaMarin315, AureliaM555, or any combination

A positive, professional photo of yourself for your avatar is a smart contribution to an effective home page.

of initials, names, and numbers. Check and see how your favorite bloggers use their names for professional purposes. Using your real name trades anonymity for accessibility. You want people to know who you are.

Once you have confirmed your account by email, it is time to customize your home page. Start by choosing a theme. The theme you choose will depend on your goals for your site. Some themes are more suited for text, others for photos or artwork. If your site will have both, then look for a theme that allows for multiple layouts and is not too fussy. You do not need to pay for a good theme, as there are plenty of free ones that can suit your purpose. You can change your theme later if it is not working for you, but that may confuse your followers.

For your avatar, you can upload a photo of yourself looking your best, or you can use a logo that represents your purpose. Use your title to briefly explain your goals for the site, so viewers know what to look for. Look online for tips on how to use the tools Tumblr provides for adding content, using tags effectively. *Unwrapping Tumblr* is an informative blog to follow for tips and tools.

CHAPTER THREE

Learners Central

Though Tumblr is a great place to show off mastery of an art or craft and celebrate achievements in other areas, it is also a perfect place to learn and practice. Many bloggers post not just their products, but also their process. They are willing to interact with other bloggers, offering tips and mentoring. Colleges have also become enthusiastic contributors. Prospective applicants can gain insight into places where they might learn and grow.

 ## CROWDSOURCE YOUR RESEARCH

A popular activity for students is to use Tumblr to gather opinions and experiences from fellow bloggers for school projects. At any one time you can find surveys about gender roles, the impact of social media, race and ethnicity, and favorite types of pizza.

Tumblr uses tags to categorize posts. Tags are extremely important when blogging on Tumblr. Tags are the way people find your posts when they do a search. The more tags you have, the more you are defining your content. For instance, if you have been photographing eagles, you might tag your posts #eagles. However, someone searching for that tag might be looking for a band or a football team. Adding #bald, #wild," and #photography will help searchers find your photos. Only the first twenty tags on a post will show up in searches, so there is no point in using more.

Some tags for a survey might include #project, #survey, or #please help. If you decide that you want to try a survey, make sure you take a look at surveys from other bloggers. You can learn how to structure good questions and write appeals for help that will persuade bloggers to respond.

 ## MAKE A PORTFOLIO FOR COLLEGE

Career counselors say it is never too early to plan for postsecondary education, whether it's college, trade school, art school, or the military. About one third of colleges use social media to make decisions about admission prospects. What better way to impress admission officials than by creating an easily accessible portfolio that shows you at your best?

Some Tumblr users post their images directly on their homepage. This makes the images accessible, but you won't be able to use the homepage as a blog. A better choice is to make secondary pages for your portfolio. Click on the Account icon at the top of your homepage. Click on the +New icon, and a "Create a new blog" box comes up. Add a descriptive title, such as "Weekend Girlwear" or "JewelryPassion." The URL will just be your title with .tumblr.com at the end. Click "Create blog," and you're done. You can begin adding your art, photography, animation, comics, GIFs, music, and whatever else you are showcasing. Check out as many online portfolios as you can to get ideas about how to arrange yours.

EXPLAIN YOURSELF

Many people associate blogging with long text posts. Tumblr bloggers write plenty of text, but the posts tend to be shorter. Many Tumblr users use the site for musing about different topics, recording thoughts and feelings, or sounding off. Tumblr is perfect for those sorts of posts, but the site can do so much more.

Tumblr users can access their accounts on laptops, tablets, and cell phones, making it easy to add content on the fly.

You can use Tumblr to start your college admission essay. College essays tend to be intensely personal experience stories, a genre that should connect with Tumblr readers. If you are not confident about your writing skills, your Tumblr blog is a great place to practice. There is always an audience for thought-provoking pieces on the controversies of our times. You might want to explain your goals and ask for specific feedback. Unfortunately, not everyone will be as respectful as you would hope. However, teens that have their eyes on success will not let their emotions rule and participate in flame wars, where bloggers insult and argue with each other publically.

There is a wealth of resources for writing dynamite essays on Tumblr. Search using the tags with "college essay," including "tips," "advice," or "help." Like or follow the blogs that seem helpful.

FORMATTING TEXT ON TUMBLR

No one wants pages and pages of text on their Tumblr feed. It is easy to make your text posts attractive and readable. To begin, click on the Text Post icon. Highlighting a section brings up the formatting tools. An important tool is the "Read more" link. Long text pieces take up valuable space on your site, so it can show the first paragraph and hide the rest until your readers click the "Keep reading" link. You can find this tool by skipping a line and then hitting the Enter key. A small circle with a + sign will appear. You can also add photos, GIFs, or videos to your piece.

Add tags so that essay writers and those interested in your topics can find your piece. When you are ready to post, you have an option to save your piece as a draft. This gives you time to check over your work before publishing it live.

LEARN FROM THE BEST

Although your main goal may be to promote yourself, take advantage of the wealth of expertise that is on Tumblr. Whatever your passion, there are bloggers on Tumblr who can help you take it to the next level.

There are several options for searching. Just typing in a term such as "garden" brings up a menu of possibilities such as "garden diy," "garden design," and "organic garden." Below that on the page are specific blogs such as *Garden of Vegan*, *The New York Botanical Garden*, and *Garden Science*. The more tags you include, the narrower your search, and the more you will be able to find just

Tumblr users can find whole communities of people who want to connect to share their interests.

what you are looking for. For instance, adding the tag "homeless" brings up a page of bloggers who were tending gardens with and for homeless people.

Since Tumblr is also a social networking site, make sure you interact with the blogs. Like and follow them. You have a few options for talking to bloggers. When you re-blog you can add a comment. Read some typical comments by clicking on the "Notes" link on the bottom of a post. You can click on the paper airplane icon to send a message to a blogger. If someone sends you a message, you will find it in your in-box, which is the envelope icon on your dash. Also on your dash is the instant messaging icon, which is the smiling balloon. This is a fun way to interact with new Tumblr friends, and it offers more privacy than speaking through public posts.

 ## SCHOOL SUCCESS

Teens are flocking to Tumblr, so it is no surprise that school has a huge presence. There are numerous resources that can help you be more successful now and plan your next steps.

Many Tumblr bloggers have turned studying into an art. Search any form of the word "study" and you'll find practical tips, advice, and inspiration to shake up old habits and routines that may not be working for you anymore. Some popular blogs include photos of study schedules and chemistry notes transformed with design and color into works of art.

Other bloggers are thinking beyond high school and documenting their journey through the college application process. They provide insight into what, for

Students use Tumblr to pass on study tips and other ways to make academic life more fun and creative.

many students, is one of the hardest decisions of their lives. Check out #college admission.

It's not just students that flock to Tumblr. Colleges also have a presence there. The site #higheredsocialmedia keeps a current list of colleges and universities that use Tumblr as a marketing tool. Students can see a side of college life that doesn't show up in catalogs or on websites.

Another difficult decision for many college-bound students is choosing a major. Tumblr delivers here as well. Following other teens as they search for interests inside themselves and outside their comfort zones can be inspiring. You can search for specific majors or just #collegemajor to find their stories. Share your own story to find motivation and encouragement.

CHAPTER FOUR

Authentic AND Professional!

Many teens are eager to join the work world. They want part-time jobs to save money for college. They want real-life experience in a potential occupation. They have ideas for starting their own business. Tumblr can be a great resource for teens who want a head start on a career. Today's job seekers are using social media to host innovative résumés. They are using sites such as Tumblr to showcase their interests, initiative, and resourcefulness. And they are finding that their blogging and networking skills are in hot demand.

CREATING STAND-OUT RÉSUMÉS

For job-hunting teens, an up-do-date résumé is a must. If you want to stand out from the crowd and get your résumé noticed, harness the power of Tumblr. With a Tumblr résumé, not only will you attract attention to your skills and experience, you will be demonstrating your social media savvy.

You can get résumé advice at #resume. Once you have an accurate, readable traditional résumé, post it on a separate page on your Tumblr. Then use Tumblr tools to express your talents and expertise for potential employers to see. You can create a YouTube video to introduce yourself. You can post quotes to express your values. Photos can show your accomplishments in sports, academics, or extracurricular activities. You might want to include writing samples or a Q&A to show your personality. Just be sure to remove your address and phone number from the résumé to avoid being contacted by people with less-than-admirable intentions.

If you want to attract employers to your blog, make sure your presence is professional. Don't have any profanity, spelling or grammar mistakes, or mentions of alcohol or drugs. Do include posts about your membership in clubs, sports teams you have played on, and recommendations from teachers or youth leaders.

Twenty-first century job applicants are using social media tools as extensions of their traditional résumés.

Search, like, follow, and re-blog any interesting résumés you find on Tumblr. It is possible to link your Tumblr to your Facebook or Twitter accounts. Only consider this if these accounts are as professional as your Tumblr and have privacy settings in place to protect your more sensitive information.

 ## DOCUMENT VOLUNTEERISM

Have you ever considered volunteering? Or maybe you already spend time working for a cause? Sharing this passion is a great way to showcase your cause. Teens all over the world dish up dinners for the homeless, care

for dogs and cats at animal shelters, spend spring break building houses for disadvantaged families, and working on hundreds of other socially conscious activities without compensation. Some even take a gap year before college. Check out #volunteer stories, #gap year, and #dosomething.

If you are ready to begin but not sure where to volunteer, Tumblr is full of ideas.

Tumblr users can find inspiring stories of teens who have documented their experiences volunteering, working on causes, or traveling.

EMPLOYERS DO CHECK SOCIAL MEDIA

When employers hire new employees, they want to find out as much about the job applicants as they can before they make a job offer. They are limited by what the applicants choose to reveal about themselves on their applications and in interviews. Many employers are using social media as a window into their applicants' lives. For instance, Tracy Brisson, CEO of talent development company The Opportunities Project, admitted on the digital media website Mashable that she monitored a job applicant's social media profile "for about three weeks and saw what she was doing on Tumblr, Twitter, etc. to evaluate her marketing effectiveness and if her style matched what I wanted." Such practices are becoming increasingly common, especially if social media, marketing, or communication is part of the role being filled.

Technology experts advise teens and young adults to pay close attention to their social media accounts. Do not let anyone tag you on anything that compromises your reputation. Set your privacy settings to just close friends and family. Your social media presence should reflect your personality, with a G rating. If you are unsure if something is OK for social media, it's best to be safe and keep it to yourself. Once it's been posted, even deleted posts can be accessed with just a little savvy.

Job applicants need to make sure that all of their social media accounts portray a professional image.

On one search, there appeared invitations to volunteer at the Monterey Bay Aquarium in California, on a Virginia goat farm, at an Oklahoma library story hour, and for a group who knits hats for cancer patients in Michigan. Scrolling through the posts will provide ideas about dozens of places and organizations in your own community that you could contact about volunteering.

Once you have committed yourself and become involved in a cause, you can use Tumblr to record your experiences. Post photos and stories of your activities and reflections about them. This documentation will be a valuable way to become aware of your growth as a person. You can identify skills that transfer to the workforce. You can also look for hints of where your college or career path might lead. Most volunteers realize that though they are working for someone or something else, they are the main beneficiaries.

 ## MARKET YOUR WORKPLACE

Tumblr may have helped you find employment. But has your employer found Tumblr? If your business, organization, church, or club doesn't have a presence on Tumblr, you might be the perfect person for the job. Often all an organization or business needs is an employee with a good understanding of a platform; they are happy to gain exposure but do not know where to start. That's where you can help.

Tumblr can be an effective platform for your employer or volunteer site. As business reporter Lauren Drell says, "With the popularity of Tumblr and the ease of setting up, customizing and maintaining your blog, we suggest you at least check it out — there's a very engaged Tumblr audience waiting to see your content."

Tumblr bloggers don't want to see ads or commercials, Drell advises. Instead, give the Tumblr audience a behind-the-scenes look at the business or organization, sneak peeks of new products, and short anecdotes about the principal people involved. The Tumblr audience is young, geeky, and hip, with money and time to spend. Take a look at what a corporate restaurant such as Denny's has done with fun and quirky content that catches the eye of a younger demographic through social media, especially Tumblr.

Tumblr users often use the site to check out companies and products they are interested in to see what's new and exciting.

There are a few important considerations when using Tumblr on behalf of an organization. First, use effective marketing strategies. You can find good examples by searching for the brands and organizations you love. Model your blogs after the ones you like. Another concern is making sure you represent the brand of your employer accurately and as they prefer. Get approval for every post before you publish it. But most important, use the skills you already deploy on your own behalf. You won't just be having fun; the title "social media manager" will look great on your résumé.

FOLLOW THOUGHT LEADERS IN YOUR FIELD

Many people credit their success to finding and following thought leaders in their field to help them develop their ideas. These are people who make an impact, have an innovative perspective, and can show you new ways of looking at the world. Tumblr is full of bloggers who are inspirational to their followers.

Successful beauty industry leader Michelle Phan was a nineteen-year-old restaurant server when she started using social media to blog about make-up. Through her videos and other media, she has since started a lifestyle network and has created her own beauty brand. Another blogger, Marie Forleo, has helped millions of people as a life and career coach. A number of fashion bloggers—including Nicola Formichetti, Cynthia Rowley, and Coco Rocha—have huge audiences who enjoy the behind-the-scenes peeks at the fashion world. They

Michelle Phan leveraged her enormous social media fan base into a beauty empire of make-up products, book contracts, and a video channel.

create product partnerships and land contracts based on their connection with their sizeable following.

If beauty and fashion aren't your concern, know that Tumblr is full of socially conscious and thought-provoking communities. Thought-provoking social justice blogs have a home on Tumblr. Journalist, TV host, and transgender activist Janet Mock posts about race, gender, culture, and authenticity. Actress and activist Amandla Stenberg, who gained fame with the "Don't Cash Crop My Cornrows" video she created for a school project, is vocal on Tumblr about social justice. The blog *Reclaiming the Latina* celebrates the diversity of Latina culture; such sites are common and give voice to perspectives that may be difficult to bring to the fore on other platforms.

You can also find your favorite authors on Tumblr. The Tumblr site *YA Highway* provides a directory. The authors often have tips for budding fiction writers and poets. Other great sites for writers who are also readers are *Diversity in YA, Gay YA,* and *YARN: The Young Adult Review Network.*

You will find that leaders may be organizations as well as individuals. Any business or nonprofit organization that leads in real life will most likely have a Tumblr presence as well. Each year members of NaNoWriMo (National Novel Writing Month) communities attempt to write a novel over the course of November, with writers of varying backgrounds and levels of experience supporting each other. While NaNoWriMo is an organization devoted to promoting writing practice, it finds a whole new life on Tumblr through this active community.

CHAPTER FIVE

Channel Your Passion

Though there are dark areas and unkind people, Tumblr is most often a place of positivity. Bloggers create, follow, and re-blog posts that celebrate diverse points of view. They also celebrate themselves and each other. In a 2014 interview with *USA Today*, Tumblr founder David Karp said his goal is to build a site with "something for everybody. Diversity of ages, geography and gender, religion and race, and sexuality—everybody is represented here." This commitment is reflected in the variety of content available on the platform, and you can find people to connect with who are just like you or of wildly different backgrounds and views.

 FIND CAUSES YOU SUPPORT AND SUPPORT CAUSES IN WHICH YOU BELIEVE

With its millions of bloggers and billions of posts, it is safe to say that anyone can find a community on Tumblr.

The company says that 64 percent of users care about social causes and look into them on Tumblr. Many bloggers use their presence to support the causes about which they are passionate.

Venezuelan-American actor Dylan Marron was discouraged by the lack of diversity in the Hollywood film industry. He used his eye-opening Tumblr blog to post edits of well-known films with everything cut away except the words spoken by a person of color. Debbie Reese, a Pueblo Indian woman, uses her blog to examine the way indigenous peoples are portrayed in children's and young adult books. *Free LGBTQPIA* lists free books, videos, and more about lesbian, gay, bisexual, transgender, questioning, pansexual, poly-sexual, intersex and asexual identity and issues.

Tumblr is a great way to connect and organize with others to become active supporters of the causes in which you believe.

If you feel strongly about a cause, search for it on Tumblr. Try these: #racism, #equality, #oppression, #feminism. As a part of what the media has called hashtag activism, you can join a socially conscious group by following it through social media accounts of organizations and users organized around specific hashtags for events, causes, or news. You may also want to start a socially conscious blog and invite others to join it. Create a secondary page from your main blog. Then click the Members icon and type in the email addresses of people you'd like to help you curate or create content for the blog. Your friends will receive an email with instructions to join this blog and register if they are not Tumblr users yet. Not only will you be able to support your cause, you will get practical experience with leadership as you manage contributions and interact with the followers of your blog.

Social media users can find on Tumblr whole groups of people with whom they have had very little experience. Some teens grow up in communities with little diversity. They may be struggling themselves with feelings of loneliness and alienation because they are perceived to be different. They find on Tumblr people they can relate to and share experiences with. Many users say that they find acceptance in one or more of the subcultures on the site. One Tumblr user told an ABC reporter in 2015, "We are a melting pot of individuals who deserve to have a voice."

Some of the most interesting places are where different groups find they interconnect. For instance, the *Black Girl Dangerous* blog calls itself the "Intersection of race, gender and sexuality." *The Brown Queer*

People of all backgrounds and ethnicities can find a safe, supportive place to make connections on Tumblr.

Project says that it "focuses on making the lives of queer and trans people of color (QTPOC) more visible." Users post about being an autistic feminist or disabled gay person. As people with different backgrounds talk about their lives, others come to understand these different perspectives. Sometimes they may understand themselves better. "I see many more diverse images on Tumblr than I see anywhere else. It's one of the

few places where I see fat people, trans women and trans women of color who are celebrated," a Tumblr user told *New York Times* reporter Valeriya Safronova.

 CALL TO ACTION

Many Tumblr users are content to contribute relevant content to their blog about an issue or cause. They may actively follow and re-blog related posts, amassing followers who sympathize. Other users, however, may want to do more. They may want to use their blog to make positive changes to their community. Once you identify a small world of users who share your concerns, you can duplicate the ways that successful bloggers have made a difference.

If you are going to exercise leadership in the area of your concern, you should become an authority in that field. Make sure you do your research and listen to experts in the field. Tumblr blogs often provide links to historical and current events websites that provide deep background on many issues. To bring different perspectives to your blog, you might interview someone who is involved and has authority and knowledge about your issue. You can post the interview as a video, an audio file, or text.

Teens can use Tumblr to practice leadership skills. They can become experts on a cause and use their blogs to inspire followers to work for social change.

Adding your thoughts and sharing different perspectives on the issues will allow you to provide a source of balanced information for your followers.

It is important to bring attention to the causes you and your Tumblr audience find important. But you can do more. A clear call to action can galvanize your audience to become involved as well. Ask your audience to contact their elected representatives, write emails of support, vote, participate in community events, or offer their services when needed. Providing concrete

EFFECTIVE HASHTAG ACTIVISM: BLACK LIVES MATTER

Tumblr's internal surveys show that 64 percent of users care about social causes and look to the site for information, reports Valeriya Safronova of the *New York Times.* The Black Lives Matter movement born on social media is one of these causes. It became an important movement in 2013 following the acquittal of George Zimmerman in the shooting of African American teen Trayvon Martin. In 2014, community organizer and Tumblr blogger Mwende Katwiwa promoted a Black Lives Matter protest in New Orleans. Four hundred people showed up. Blogger Kim Moore used Tumblr to organize a similar event in San Diego. "I was blown away at how engaged and how passionate people can be on Tumblr," she told Safronova.

Someone wanting to become an authority on this movement might research other conflicts involving racial minorities and law enforcement, as well as previous civil rights movements. Combing historical context with social action is an effective way to bring people together to combat issues.

steps toward action and a specific goal will help your followers take up action to support your causes. Once you've got your message out into the world, be sure to thank your followers for their support.

CHAPTER SIX

Express Your Best Self

Tumblr has carved out its own niche in the online world as a platform that meets many needs. Some bloggers appreciate the site most for its culture of acceptance. Many would argue that its supportive and energetic culture and its numerous subcultures are Tumblr's best features.

Teens who sometimes feel anonymous and voiceless can find like-minded friends in the many fandom communities on Tumblr. Film, TV, literature, comic books, and video games are the source of many fan groups, though they can also congregate around food, fitness, fashion, and cute animals. Tumblr is well-known for its fanfiction content.

With its many ways to create and curate content, Tumblr welcomes self-expression of all sorts. With so many options, it can seem overwhelming to dive into the site, so starting with a specific community can feel a bit more manageable.

WRITING FANFIC

Fanfiction is hugely popular on Tumblr. If you have ever wondered what would happen if Draco Malfoy had a crush on Hermione Granger, there are stories that provide different ideas. In its annual "Year in Review" for 2015, Tumblr listed Captain Swan, a "ship" or relationship between Captain Hook and Emma Swan of the TV program *Once Upon a Time* as one of its most popular pairings. Would you like to try writing fanfic yourself?

First you need to choose your source material and make sure you know the fictional universe well. If you can't decide between two sources, try a crossover story. Read fanfic to get a sense of how writers use the sources. You might begin with "drabbles," pieces less than one hundred words in length. Or you can write new characters into an existing universe, using them as a jumping-off point for your own story.

Start with an outline. A story arc contains an opening conflict, plot development with high and low points, and a resolution that makes sense.

Fanfic authors recommend giving your story to a beta reader, who can provide feedback to improve the piece. Find blogs that provide helpful tips and advice. Authors such as J. K. Rowling encourage fanfiction as long as no one is trying to sell their work. However, some authors consider fanfic to be copyright infringement and don't allow it. Become informed by following your favorite fanfic authors.

Author J. K. Rowling encourages Harry Potter fans to show their love for the characters by writing fan fiction.

JOIN THE FANDOM

Tumblr hosts wildly diverse communities. Some are so big and active they become subcultures. Fandoms are perhaps Tumblr's most loyal participants. Users have created mini-universes based on favorite stories, characters, celebrities, games, and other residents of pop culture. These fandoms have produced fan art, fanfiction, and avid discussions about the fan worlds.

Internet news site the Daily Dot calculates the most popular fandoms of each year. *Star Wars*, *Harry Potter, Dr. Who*, and Marvel TV programs seem to be perennially popular. The hit Broadway show *Hamilton* took off with fans after it opened in 2015. The success of the Mars program run by the US space agency, NASA, plus the hit Matt Damon film *The Martian* directed a lot of audience attention to the red planet. You are sure to find a fan group for your popular culture passion.

Fandom has its own language on Tumblr. Most fans engage in fanfiction, or fanfic. Fans take stories and characters from TV, film, or books and use them to create their own stories. Some writers use the canon, meaning every person and event in the real story, and then make an alternate universe where they insert themselves. For instance, you might want to attend Hogwarts and go off on new adventures with Harry Potter. If Harry meets up with Sherlock Holmes, that situation would be considered a xover, or crossover. Fans sometimes meet up IRL, or in real life, at cons, or conventions.

For readers and writers, fandoms are outlets for creativity and community. Although negative and hurtful comments can be found on any online platform, for the most part fans find acceptance, encouragement, and support.

CELEBRATE SELF-EXPRESSION

Imagination reigns on Tumblr. Your creativity is only limited by the amount of time you have to spend. While trends come and go on the internet, original artwork, photography, GIFs, fiction, poetry, and comics consistently claim audiences and zip around the online world at the speed of light. Tumblr supports authors and artists open to new forms of expression. These pieces

GIVE A TUMBLR GIFT

Do you need a special gift for the special people in your life but have an empty wallet? You can create a private Tumblr blog filled with content chosen just for them. First, create a secondary blog and give it a personal URL, such as "happybirthdaymom40. tumblr.com." Select the "Password protect this blog" option and create a personalized password. Select your settings icon and click on the new blog's name. Scroll down to the Privacy Settings and uncheck the "allow this blog to appear in search results" option. Customize the blog with your avatar and a theme. Now you are ready to begin posting the content that will make your blog recipient smile. Original content that has meaning for both of you will have the greatest impact. Send them the URL and password and get ready to celebrate.

Many teens use Tumblr as a private space to record their thoughts and feelings about their lives.

of content are the lifeblood of Tumblr; if you choose to focus on re-blogging content you love, make sure to include the artist or author's attribution.

If you want to focus on creating your own posts, scroll through the trending blogs to see what users are doing that seems interesting or inventive. Use different posts as inspiration to see how you can learn and grow in various forms of self-expression. You might try new ways to use your camera or rework a story idea as a comic. Instead of automatically clicking on Texts to begin a poem, click on Photos instead, and recreate the emotional feel of your idea through images. If you normally work with street-style fashion, try vintage or boho, or move into make-up or interior design.

You'll find infinite sources of inspiration on Tumblr. Giving credit where it is due is an important part of the Tumblr culture. If you re-create an image you love, make sure you link to the original. Tumblr users are good at picking up on plagiarism and won't hesitate to point out if they think work has been taken without crediting the creator.

IMPROVE YOUR MENTAL HEALTH WITH A JOURNAL

As a blogging and social media platform, Tumblr is all about sharing. However, it can function as a private place for people to explore their interior lives. Keeping a journal on Tumblr makes a lot of sense. Tumblr's mobile app keeps your journal anywhere your phone is, which is probably never far away. You can easily create a secondary site that you password protect. You are not limited to text, but can add images, video, or music to express your inner self.

Perhaps the best reason for journaling on Tumblr is the boost to your mental health that comes from regularly recording your thoughts and emotions. Health experts say that journaling can help you clarify your thoughts and feelings, especially when you feel confused. Writing about strong emotions, such as anger or frustration, helps release the intensity of these feelings. Rather than obsessing over misunderstandings, writing helps you get them out of your system so you can move on to more productive thoughts.

Many writers find it liberating to write just for themselves, without worrying about correctness or feedback. While you might be tempted to let your journal loose on Tumblr, you will benefit more if you keep this just for yourself. It can become the wellspring of creativity for the rest of your Tumblr life. But you don't want to put yourself in the position of having to censor yourself for an audience or writing something you later regret. Password protecting and setting your blog to private will create a space where you can speak your mind freely, which is the best way to get in touch with your emotions and thoughts.

CHAPTER SEVEN

Time Management 101

T umblr's imaginative, hilarious, heart-breaking, and thought-proving content can make users lose themselves for hours, possibly jeopardizing homework, family time, and physical activity. It is important to set priorities and time limits when on Tumblr. It is also essential to follow the rules on Tumblr, both written and unwritten. The Community Guidelines protect both freedom of speech and freedom from malicious speech and harassment. Tumblr calls itself "a global platform for creativity and self-expression." The Tumblr team of developers and engineers hope that users take time to appreciate and be a part of the sheer fun and cleverness of Tumblr.

Any teen who has had to juggle school, homework, sports, youth groups, extracurricular activities, family

Many Tumblr users share different strategies that help teens organize their busy lives. Calendars are great tools to keep track of commitments.

commitments, internships, and a volunteer or paying job, knows about time management. People with a lot on their plate become good at organizing their life. They identify their goals and prioritize their time so that important steps to their goals get done. They use calendars, planners,

and to-do lists. These organizational tools become essential as they move from high school to postsecondary education or careers.

One key to success in any endeavor is breaking large goals down and committing to smaller daily, weekly, and monthly goals. You can document your progress toward your goals on your Tumblr and ask your friends and followers to hold you accountable toward meeting your goals. Apps such as GoalsOnTrack, Smart Goals, Stickk, or LifeTick can also help you stay on track. There are whole communities devoted to maximizing these practices, often called "#life hacks."

You have probably realized that it is easy to lose track of time on Tumblr. Happy, successful people live a balanced life prioritizing their family, friends, and health with enough time for work, school, and leisure. Activities such as shooting hoops with friends, having dinner with your family, completing homework assignments, and getting device-free rest will benefit you more than tending to anonymous friends on social media. Use a computer or phone app such as StayFocusd to set a limit on how much time you will spend. In your Settings menu, you can also disable endless scrolling, which may help you set a limit on clicks.

Many Tumblr users are tempted to chase popularity, acquiring as many notes and followers as they can. It is possible, but unlikely, that one of your posts could go viral and you then become instantly famous. Most popular bloggers such as Madisen Kuhn and Brandon Stanton spent years creating original content and curating their sites. You can find strategies and tips on how to increase your popularity, but as happens in school, you often find yourself compromising your values for dubious rewards.

GIFS

You have probably noticed that GIFs are a huge part of Tumblr. Though many people joke that the acronym stands for great internet fun, it actually comes from "graphics interchange format." These flashy animated images debuted on the internet in 1987 and suited early websites more easily than video. They attracted more attention than static art. Their popularity waxed and waned until GIF-friendly platforms such as Tumblr were created to showcase creative animations.

Sometimes the animation itself is clever. Sometimes the GIFs are paired with ingenious captions that give them their inspired edge. Often GIFs are pulled from memorable scenes from movies or television, but they can be animated photographs or original art as well. You can try making your own GIFs using free programs found on the internet.

Stay focused on your goals and be true to yourself, and the followers will come.

 ## FOLLOW THE RULES

Anyone who has ever played sports knows that following the rules of the game results in more fun. All rules, Tumblr's included, begin with respect. Respect yourself by posting with integrity, and respect others by acknowledging their rights to a safe, enjoyable experience on Tumblr.

The Community Guidelines are found by clicking the Help icon and then looking under Policy. They are listed under the title "What Tumblr is not for." The first set of guidelines concern safety, both physical and psychological. Site managers are aware that a large percentage of users are teens and young adults. They warn against malicious speech by saying, "Being a teenager is complicated enough without the anxiety, sadness and isolation caused by bullying."

New York Times writer Valeriya Safronova reported that, in 2014, college student Amanda Levitt, who moderates a blog called *This is Thin Privilege*, received over four thousand negative comments, some even suggesting she should die. Participating in hateful speech and engaging in a flame war creates negative energy that distracts from your purpose. Tumblr suggests that you respond to negative comments with humor or a clever GIF, which is the last thing that the commenters expect. You can also block users who are sending unwanted messages or re-blogs by opening the user's avatar and selecting "Block."

One of the important functions of the Community Guidelines is safety. The site does not want users to promote or glorify self-harm. This means not posting content that encourages eating disorders, cutting, or suicide. Instead, it offers a page of Counseling and Prevention Resources, found by clicking the Help icon.

Other guidelines concern content. Tumblr asks that users don't deceptively add tags that don't relate to content, just to drive traffic to your content. Tumblr is particularly concerned about copyright infringement. It is illegal to pass off someone else's work as your own. If you post a photo you didn't take, a poem you didn't write, or a GIF you didn't create, you have to identify the source. If you don't, you can be sure that someone will notice and send a complaint.

For every infringement of the guidelines, Tumblr provides a link to a complaint form. After sending it in, a Tumblr team member will contact you to follow up. Remember that, when it comes to your online presence, nothing is more valuable than your reputation. Protect it.

HAVE FUN

Social media was invented because humans have an instinctual need to connect. Brain research is beginning to show what everyone who shares online already knows. Connection feels good. Also part of being human is accessing imagination and expressing creativity. It is no wonder that a social media platform that facilitates both of these activities is so popular.

Do your best to maximize your time on Tumblr. Use it to achieve your goals. Become better at your craft, learn from the masters, spotlight your accomplishments, and make connections with people who can help you. But do these activities in ways that nourish you as a person. What does this mean? Don't engage with negativity. Don't waste your time. Do approach each session with an open mind. As the Tumblr team advises, "We want you to express yourself freely and use Tumblr to reflect who you are, and what you love, think, and stand for." Let yourself be surprised by what you find on Tumblr and work to surprise other users. Most of all, surprise yourself.

GLOSSARY

acronym A word formed from the first letters of a set phrase.

algorithm A set of rules for solving a mathematical problem.

anecdote A short account of a particular event.

avatar An image that represents a person.

beneficiary A person who receives benefits, profits, or advantages.

canon The official or established storyline of a creative work.

compensation Payment for work or services.

curate To sift through and select for presentation.

dubious Of doubtful quality.

entrepreneur A person who organizes a business, usually with initiative and risk.

flame An angry, critical, or mean post or comment.

harassment Repeated disturbing, pestering, or bothering behavior.

infringement Breaking the law or violating an obligation.

malicious Harmful, spiteful, or vicious.

marketing The process of promoting and selling a product or service.

memes Ideas, behaviors, styles, or usage that spreads from person to person within a culture.

niche A job or activity that is suitable for someone.

nonprofit Not existing or done for the purpose of making a profit.

perennially Lasting for a long time.

savvy Having practical know-how.

Berkman Klein Center for Internet and Society
Harvard University
3 Everett Street, 2nd Floor
Cambridge, MA 02138
(617) 495-7547
Website: https://cyber.law.harvard.edu/
The Berkman Klein Center represents a network of
faculty, students, fellows, entrepreneurs, lawyers,
and virtual architects working to identify and
engage with the challenges and opportunities
of cyberspace.

Common Sense Media
650 Townsend, Suite 435
San Francisco, CA 94103
(415) 863-0600
Website: https://www.commonsensemedia.org/
The mission of Common Sense Media is to empower
parents, teachers, and policymakers by providing
information, advice, and tools to use media wisely.
It helps students make smart choices when using
digital media.

Cyberbullying
National Crime Prevention Council
2001 Jefferson Davis Highway, Suite 901
Arlington, VA 22202
(202) 466-6272
Website: http://www.ncpc.org/cyberbullying
This organization provides explanations, tips, and
resources for teens who are victims of cyberbullying
or just want more information.

Media Smarts
950 Gladstone Avenue, Suite 120
Ottawa, ON K1Y 3E6
Canada
(613) 224-7721
Website: http://mediasmarts.ca
Media Smarts is a nonprofit organization that provides
    digital and media literacy. Its goal is to teach
    children and teens the critical thinking skills needed
    to become active and informed digital citizens.

StopBullying.gov
200 Independence Avenue SW
Washington, DC 20201
(877) 696-6775
Website: www.stopbullying.gov
StopBullying.gov is a federal government website
    that explains what bullying is and what children,
    teens, parents, and educators can do to prevent it.
    It provides resources to assist teens in dealing with
    cyberbullying and using technology safely.

WEBSITES

Because of the changing nature of internet links, Rosen
Publishing has developed an online list of websites
related to the subject of this book. This site is updated
regularly. Please use this link to access the list:

http://www.rosenlinks.com/SMCB/tumblr

FOR FURTHER READING

Bair, Amy Lupold, and Susannah Gardner. *Blogging for Dummies*. Hoboken NJ: John Wiley & Sons, 2014.

Berlatsky, Noah. *Are Social Networking Sites Harmful?* (At Issue). Farmington Hills, MI: Greenhaven Press, 2014.

Boyd, Danah. *It's Complicated: The Social Lives of Networked Teens*. New Haven, CT: Yale University Press, 2014.

Jackson, Aurelia. *How David Karp Changed the Way We Blog* (Wizards of Technology). Broomall, PA: Mason Crest, 2015.

Kenney, Karen Latchana. *David Karp, the Mastermind Behind Tumblr*. Minneapolis, MN: Lerner Publications Company, 2013.

Obee, Jenna. *Social Networking: The Ultimate Teen Guide* (It Happened to Me). Lanham, MA: Scarecrow Press, 2012.

Sales, Nancy Jo. *American Girls: Social Media and the Secret Lives of Teenagers*. New York, NY: Alfred A. Knopf, 2016.

Salpeter, Miriam. *Social Networking for Career Success*. New York, NY: Learning Express, 2013.

Schwartz, Heather. *Safe Social Networking* (Tech Safety Smarts). North Mankato, MN: Captstone, 2013.

Small, Cathleen. *Make the Most of Tumblr and Other Blogging Platforms* (Web Wisdom). New York, NY: Cavendish Square, 2015.

Vescia, Monique. *David Karp and Tumblr* (Internet Biographies). New York, NY: Rosen Publishing Group, 2013.

Vescia, Monique. *Social Network-Powered Employment Opportunities* (A Teen's Guide to the Power of Social Networking). New York, NY: Rosen Publishing Group, 2014.

BIBLIOGRAPHY

Baig, Edward. "Tumblr's David Karp on Social Media, YouTube, Diversity." *USA TODAY*, November 4, 2014 (http://www.usatoday.com/story/tech/columnist/baig/2014/11/04/tumblr-david-karp-talks-socialmedia -diversity/18406825/).

Community Guidelines. Tumblr.com, January 26, 2015.

Drell, Lauren. "The Quick and Dirty Guide to Tumblr for Small Business." *Mashable,* February 18, 2012 (http://mashable.com/2012/02/18/tumblr-small-biz-guide/#c3s.05Y9wkqu).

Helmrich, Brittney. "Tumblr for Business: Everything You Need to Know." *Business News Daily*, January 7, 2016 (http://www.businessnewsdaily.com/7455-tumblr-for -business.html).

Hernandez, Brian. "10 Creative Social Media Resumes to Learn From." *Mashable*, May 20, 2011 (http://mashable .com/2011/05/20/social-media-resumes/#pLOF_ Gdzliqo).

Jackson, Aurelia. *Tumblr: How David Karp Changed the Way We Blog* (Wizards of Technology). Broomall, PA: Mason Crest, 2015.

Kamenetz, Anya. "The Writing Assignment That Changes Lives." NPR, July 10, 2015 (http://www.npr.org/sections/ed/2015/07/10/419202925/the-writing-assignment-that -changes-lives).

Moreau, Elise. "The Rise of the Animated GIF." About Tech, February 9, 2015 (http://webtrends.about.com/od/Gifs/a/Animated-Gif.htm).

O'Dell, Jolie. *Blogging for Photographers: Explore Your Creativity and Build Your Audience.* New York, NY: Focal Press, 2013.

Reeve, Elspeth. "The Secret Lives of Tumbler Teens." *New Republic,* February 17, 2016 (https://newrepublic.com/article/129002/secret-lives-tumblr-teens).

Rogers, Katie. "Meet Tumblr's 15-Year-Old Secret Keeper."
    New York Times, November 30, 2015 (http://www
    .nytimes.com/2015/12/01/style/meet-tumblrs-15-year-old
    -secret-keeper.html?_r=0).
Safronova, Valeriya. "Millennials and the Age of Tumblr
    Activism" *New York Times*, December 19, 2014 (http://
    www.nytimes.com/2014/12/21/style/millennials-and-the
    -age-of-tumblr-activism.html).
Schaefer, Mark, and Stanford Smith. *Born to Blog: Building
    Your Blog for Personal and Business Success, One Post
    at a Time*. New York, NY : McGraw-Hill Education, 2013.
Tan, Avianne. "#MyVanityFairCover Highlights Diversity of
    Transgender Community On Tumblr." ABCNews, June 5,
    2015 (http://abcnews.go.com/US/myvanityfaircover
    -highlights-diversity-transgender-community-tumblr/
    story?id=31534737).
Willford, Ava. "Madisen Kuhn's 'Eighteen Years:' A 2016
    Must Have." *Odyssey*, January 4, 2016 (http://
    theodysseyonline.com/ohio/madisen-kuhns-eighteen
    -years-2016/264173).
"Why Tumblr." Tumblr Business. Accessed March 4, 2016
    (www.tumblr.com/business).

INDEX

ABOUT THE AUTHOR

Susan Henneberg is the author of numerous nonfiction books written for today's tech-savvy teens and young adults. She lives and works in Reno, Nevada. A former high school teacher, she currently teaches writing at Truckee Meadows Community College.

PHOTO CREDITS

Cover Dima Sidelnikov/Shutterstock.com; p. 3 everything possible/Shutterstock.com; pp. 4–5 background solarseven/Shutterstock.com; pp. 4–5 (inset) Stan Honda/AFP/Getty Images; p. 9 Andrew Burton/Getty Images; p. 11 Anadolu Agency/Getty Images; p. 15 verity jane smith/Blend Images/Getty Images; p. 17 valentinrussanov/E+/Getty Images; p. 21 Stock-Asso/Shutterstock.com; p. 23 Peter Dazeley/Photographer's Choice/Getty Images; pp. 25, 38–39 Rawpixel.com/Shutterstockcom; p. 27 Klaus Vedfelt/Riser/Getty Images; p. 28 Anna Gorin/Moment/Getty Images; pp. 29, 31 Hero Images/Getty Images; p. 33 Dave Kotinsky/Getty Images; p. 36 a katz/Shutterstock.com; p. 40 © iStockphoto.com/sturti; p. 43 Chip Somodevilla/Getty Images; p. 46 KidStock/Blend Images/Getty Images; pp. 50–51 © iStockphoto.com/Rawpixel Ltd; interior pages checklist icon D Line/Shutterstock.com; back cover background photo Rawpixel.com/Shutterstock.com.

Designer: Michael Moy; Photo Researcher: Karen Huang